THE LIFE & TIMES OF
MUHAMMAD ALI

THE LIFE & TIMES OF

Muhammad Ali

BY
Jon E. Lewis

SIENA

This is a Siena book
Siena is an imprint of Parragon Book Service Ltd

This edition first published by
Parragon Book Service Ltd in 1996

Parragon Book Service Ltd
Unit 13–17 Avonbridge Trading Estate
Atlantic Road, Avonmouth
Bristol BS11 9QD

Produced by Magpie Books Ltd, London

ISBN 0 75251 581 0

A copy of the British Library Cataloguing in Publication
Data is available from the British Library.

Typeset by Whitelaw & Palmer Ltd, Glasgow

THE WEIGH-IN

He was more than a boxer. He was a symbol of Black Power, he was an entertainer, he was a preacher for Islam, he was a supreme athlete. He transcended boxing, and so made it the greatest show on earth. For over two decades he was the most famous, most charismatic sportsman in the world.

He was Muhammad Ali, né Cassius Clay.

He was – as he told you himself, again and

again – The Greatest.

Cassius Marcellus Clay Jr was born in Louisville, Kentucky, at 6.35 p.m. on 17 January 1942. He weighed in at 6 pounds 7 ounces. The birth was traumatic; his head was large, and had to be pulled out with forceps. The Roman noble name came, via his father, from Cassius Marcellus Clay (1810–1903), the Kentucky plantation owner, politician and sometime American Ambassador to the Court of St James's. Apparently, one of Muhammad Ali's forebears, as was common at the time, was given, or took, the name of his slavemaster since he had no other.

Muhammad Ali's mother, Odessa Lee Grady Clay, was also of slave stock, but with a dash

Muhammad Ali

of Irish. Her great-grandfather was born in County Clare, and like many a young man in the 1870s had gone west to the New World, where he had met and married a black girl.

The Clay family at the time young Cassius was growing up was poor, but not dirt poor. Cassius Clay Sr was a sign-painter, the best in Louisville, and never out of work. Odessa worked too, toiling as a cleaner in the houses of rich white women. Aside from Cassius, there was only one other child, a brother Rudy, which was a help to the family purse. The Clays had their own house – broken and ramshackle, but their own – in the black neighbourhood of West End, as well as a series of ancient, sluggish cars with bald tyres. Their clothes came from the charity, Good Will. There was, though, usually food enough to eat. And there were a lot of the things that money can't buy: love, respect, friends and good health. The Clays were tightly-knit. They still are.

Yet a more different couple than Odessa and Cassius Sr it would be hard to envisage. Odessa – or 'Bird', as young Cassius nicknamed her – was homey, God-fearing and quiet. Mr Clay was, in his son's own words, 'a hep-cat', a drinker, a girl-chaser, and a fancy-dresser. His Police Department file was sizeable. Most offences related to drunken behaviour and reckless driving.

Mr and Mrs Clay were devoted to each other, and their sons to them.

Cassius Clay Jr was a bright and able boy who walked and talked early. According to his mother, the first sounds he ever made were

'Gee. Gee.' (In retrospect, Ali says he was trying to say 'Gee. Gee. I'm the greatest', or maybe 'Golden Gloves'.) He was bright, but not academic. At Virginia Avenue Grade School and, later, Central High he did poorly, partly because of a reading difficulty, partly because he clowned around.

But as his marks went down in school, his ability at one extracurricular activity irresistibly went up. Boxing.

The story of how Cassius Clay began boxing is well known. One rainy day in October 1954 he and a best buddy went off cycling until the rain got too heavy and they decided to find some shelter. This was provided by the Louisville Home Show at the Columbia Auditorium on Louisville's Fourth and York, where the attraction – for two small boys –

was free hotdogs and free candy. While they were inside, Cassius's bike was stolen. Someone suggested they report the theft to a policeman, Joe Elsby Martin, who ran a boxing gym in the Columbia's basement. Cassius went to see Martin – and fell in love with boxing there and then. He was twelve, skinny, around 112 pounds in weight.

There was, of course, more to it than that. Cassius had long wanted to make something of himself, to be a big shot, to be rich. And there weren't many ways out of the ghetto for a black boy in the 1950s, when segregation was still in place. There was education, crime or sport. And of the many types of sport, pugilism offered the surest, quickest, richest exit. Jack Johnson, the 'Brown Bomber' Joe Louis, Archie Moore, Jersey Joe Walcott and other champion black boxers had already shown that. When Cassius Clay saw the gloves and punchbags fly in the Columbia Gym, he understood instinctively that the first exit from downtown Louisville was 'the ring'.

Within days, he was back in the Columbia Gym, sparring – and getting beaten. He carried his gloves too low and he wasn't large (yet). To offset this he started to move around, to dance, to use his legs. And he learned quickly. He became a student of boxing, and watched every fight he could. One thing he learned, above all others, was to hit without being hit back. To pull back from punches, to dodge punches. Weave, duck and bob. Soon he had a built-in radar for a punch, could see it coming almost before it was thrown. And he taught his body to be fit, to endure round after round. Every night he did two hours' training with Joe Martin, and then

Cassius Clay, aged 12

four hours at a church basement gym in the East End run by a black coach, Fred Stoner – every night, without exception.

He had natural abilities, too, the things that can't be taught. He was fast with his hands, had reflexes quicker than light, and was inherently graceful. More, as Joe Martin and Fred Stoner were soon to understand, Clay had the right psychology. He wanted to win, and everything he did was subordinated to that goal.

Soon Joe Martin booked Clay for a fight – his first official bout – on *Tomorrow's Champions*, a TV amateur boxing show, broadcast all over Kentucky. Clay's opponent was a white fighter, Ronny O'Keefe, whose name was destined only to be remembered as a footnote in history: the first person to be defeated by

Cassius Clay, who won on a split decision. It was just six weeks since he'd joined the gym.

After this victory, Joe Martin booked his new fighter on the show every week. To get himself noticed in the mass of young hopefuls Clay began to develop attention-grabbing gimmicks. Influenced by his father's sign-painting trade, he started penning slogans and poems: 'This guy must be done/I'll stop him in one.'

And how he bragged. 'Almost from my first fights,' he later recalled, 'I'd mouth off to anybody who would listen about what I was going to do to whoever I was going to fight. People would go out of their way to come and see, hoping I would get beat. When I was no more than a kid fighter, they would put me in bills because I was a drawing card.'

By 1958, only one thing threatened the inexorable rise and rise of Cassius Clay. He had tangled with a local street tough called Corky Baker – a man-mountain capable of lifting a truck from a flat stance – who had 'whupped' him a brawl. It began to gnaw at Clay's confidence: how could he be the best if he couldn't beat Corky? At the age of sixteen, Clay decided to have a showdown, Clay v Corky, not on the street, where there were no rules, but in the ring. Corky quit after two rounds, bloodied and bowed.

At the end of 180 amateur fights, Corky included, Clay had won six Kentucky State Golden Gloves tournaments, steadily moving up the weight divisions (thanks to a lot of eating and body-building: no one in his family, on either side, was the Herculean type) to light-heavyweight, weighing in at

175 pounds. In 1959 he won the National Golden Gloves and the National Amateur Athletic Union titles. The following year he won the Golden Gloves and National AAU tournaments again. For good measure he also won the Olympic trials at San Francisco's Cow Palace, beating black Army champion Allen Hudson with a hurricane of blows so strong that the referee was forced to stop the match. Cassius Clay had won the right to represent the USA as a light-heavyweight at the 1960 Rome Olympics.

There was, though, still some unfinished business in Louisville, his last year of high school. Clay graduated 367th out of a class of 391 from Central High. His diploma was inscribed only 'Certificate of Attendance'.

THE FEAT OF CLAY

Rome, the Eternal City. The eighteen-year-old Clay almost didn't make it to the 1960 Olympiad. The No. 1 amateur boxer in America was scared of flying, and had virtually to be pushed aboard the US team plane. With his feet back on terra firma, however, he discovered his bravery, and his mouth. From his first day in Italy he bragged he was going to win the gold. And even bigger things. He saw Floyd Patterson, the then heavyweight champion of the world, in the crowd at one of his fights. Clay shouted out: 'Floyd Patterson, some day I'm going to whup you. I am the greatest.' Patterson smiled and said, 'You're a good kid, keep trying, kid.'

Clay's first bout at the Pallazzo dello Sport was against a Belgian, Yvon Becaus, who didn't last until round three. Next Clay faced the Russian, Gennady Shatkov. Like the other competitors from the Communist countries, Shatkov was an amateur in name only. It was the first time that Clay had boxed someone with vastly more experience than he had. But he outjabbed him, and took the decision. Beating the Russian gave him more confidence, and he easily beat Australian Tony Madigan for a place in the finals. His opponent was Zbigniew Piertrzkowski, a Pole with over 230 bouts under his belt.

More, he was a southpaw, and Clay had little experience of left-handers.

The match began cautiously. The Pole kept his distance and Clay was perplexed by his opponent's unorthodox style. Not until near the end of round two did he figure out the solution, moving quickly in, catching the Pole with two fast blows to the face. Blood started to pour, and the Pole had to run for the rest of the round. By the bell at the end of round three, the bloodiest of the whole Olympics, the Pole was hanging on the ropes, defenceless, his face a dazed red mask.

The boy with the imperial Roman name, Cassius Marcellus was now the best amateur light-heavyweight fighter in the world. It was official.

There was only one sour note. On the day after his triumph a Russian journalist approached Clay and asked him: 'How does it feel to win something for a country where you can't eat at the same table with a white man?'

Clay responded angrily: 'Tell your readers we got *qualified* people working on that and I'm not worried about the outcome. The USA is still the best country in the world.'

In time the remark would come back to haunt him, but for now he was the carefree Olympic champion.

He flew back to America, landing at New York, gold medal around his neck, in a blaze of euphoria. He was fêted everywhere he went, and the Mayor gave him a private audience. He stayed in the Waldorf Hotel at the expense of cigarette magnate William Reynolds, a fellow Kentuckyian who was toying with the idea of managing Clay. Clay himself was also pondering his future. One day, walking into a Manhattan amusement arcade, he saw a machine which printed phoney newspaper headlines for 23 cents. The one Clay paid to have made up read: 'CASSIUS SIGNS FOR PATTERSON FIGHT'. He had made his decision. He would turn professional, and move up to the ultimate division, heavyweight.

After New York, Clay flew home to Louisville (duly decorated with huge 'Welcome Home, Cassius Clay' signs), where Reynolds's management deal was presented to him: a 10,000 dollar bonus for signing plus a guaranteed income for ten years. On the advice of his father, Clay turned down the deal. The objections of Clay Sr were two: because Reynolds was represented by Joe Martin – and the elder Clay distrusted policemen – and also because ten years was too long to be tied down to a contract.

A better deal from another source was not long in coming. Bill Faversham, a Louisville businessman and boxing fan, heard about the breakdown with Reynolds and invited the Clays to dinner. His offer was to form a syndicate of eleven Louisville millionaires who would put up $10,000 as an advance, underwrite all expenses, and give Clay a guaranteed income of $200 per month. The contract was to run for six years. In return, the businessmen took 50 per cent of all Clay's earnings. The investment proved shrewd. Between 1960 and 1966 Clay would earn them millions.

With his $10,000 Clay bought his parents a Cadillac and had their old Kentucky home repaired.

Clay had the financial backing to turn professional, but he still needed a manager. There were plenty of offers. Cus D'Amato, Floyd Patterson's manager, was interested, while legendary heavyweight boxer Rocky Marciano sent a telegram: 'YOU HAVE THE PROMISE. I CAN GIVE YOU THE GUIDANCE'. Archie Moore, ex-world champ, gave Clay a card which read: 'If you want a good, experienced manager, call me, collect.'

Before Clay could make up his mind which manager to choose, Faversham arranged his first professional fight. On 29 October 1960, Clay fought a white Virginian sheriff, Tunney

Hunsaker. He beat the redneck in six rounds but his performance was lacklustre. Faversham pressed him to get a manager. He chose Archie Moore, but Moore's reign as the manager of Cassius Clay lasted for days only. Clay could not handle the quietude of Moore's remote gym in the mountains near San Diego, California, or his long-haul strategy, which suggested that Clay would need to train for years before being 'ready', to fight seriously. Clay, impatient, quit and returned to Louisville.

During his short San Diego sojourn yet another management offer had come in, this time from Angelo Dundee, a vastly experienced Italian trainer whose stable included the ex-world light-heavyweight title-holder Willie Pastrano. Dundee had met Clay numerous times before, mostly when 'the kid' had pestered him for tips when his charges were fighting at Louisville. By December 1960 Clay was in Miami under Dundee's tutelage. It was destined to be boxing's most successful trainer-fighter partnership, greater even than that of Weill and Marciano. Dundee, astutely, did not tamper with Clay's natural style. Instead, he enhanced it, gave him a wider repertoire, and taught him by praise rather than criticism.

The improvement in Clay's ability was quick to show. His next four fights ended with knock-outs, which brought him much sporting attention. He went on to capture national attention by emulating the wrestler Gorgeous George, becoming a brazen egotist who even had the audacity to predict in which round his opponent would fall. His first such prediction was in a 1961 match in

Louisville against a barn-sized white farmer
from Utah, Lamar Clark. Clark would fall in
two rounds, prophesied Clay. And so it
proved to be – Clark was KO'd, nose broken,
in the second round. Afterwards, Clay told
the press, 'From now on they all must fall in
the round I call.' He never stopped talking.
'Can I have five minutes?' a cub reporter
asked him. 'No,' Clay replied, 'but you can
have three hours.' Boxing had never seen
anything like it.

There was, though, another, cleverer,
purpose to the egotism and prophecies. They
worked away at an opponent's mind before
the bout, wormed into his thoughts and
undermined his self-confidence. The art of
boxing is as psychological as it is physical.
Clay was beginning to learn how to win fights
before he even stepped into the ring.

Not until March 1963, thirteen fights on, did Clay get a prophecy seriously wrong, when he fought Doug Jones at New York's Madison Square Garden, the Mecca of pugilism. On TV and radio, Clay gave out his poetic prediction:

> Jones likes to mix,
> So I'll let it go six.
> If he talks jive,
> I'll cut it to five.
> And if he talks some more,
> I'll cut it to four.

Every seat was sold, something almost unknown for a non-championship fight. Entering the ring, Clay asked Jones, 'How tall are you?' 'Why do you want to know?' replied his opponent. 'So I'll know how far to step back when I knock you out in the fourth.'

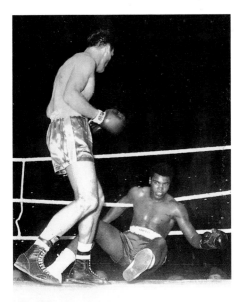

Clay falls in the Cooper fight, 1963

Jones survived the fourth. And the fifth. And the sixth. At one point he swung a right cross to Clay's jaw which caused real pain. Anybody but Clay would have gone down. He recovered to win by decision. The crowd booed him and shouted 'Fake!' On the way back to the dressing-room he had to duck missiles.

The crowd might have been unimpressed with Clay's prophetic powers, but fight promoters were awed by his audience-pulling power. Offers rolled in, including one from the English promoter Jack Solomons, to put Clay in the ring against the European champion, Henry Cooper. ' Enery', as Cooper was affectionately known, was twenty-nine, slow, a 'bleeder', but he swung what was reputed to be the best left hook in boxing.

The night of 18 June 1963 was rainy in London. Inside Wembley Stadium Clay, 207 pounds, walked to the ring amidst heralding trumpeters. On his head he wore a crown, on his back a white-trimmed scarlet bathrobe with the words 'Cassius the Greatest' across the back. His prediction was that Cooper, 'a bum and a cripple', would fall in five.

To everybody's surprise, Cooper – who weighed a light 185½ pounds – came out fighting. In round one he gave Clay a bloody nose. Three rounds on, Cooper threw the most famous punch in British boxing – a wild, vicious left hook which whipped onto Clay's chin as he paused against the ropes. It was the hardest punch Clay had ever taken. He fell back, his arms tangled in the ropes, so far gone that he did not have the sense to take the count. He got up on tottery legs. Cooper moved in for the kill.

And then the bell went. The entire course of Clay's career could have changed there and then, except for that saving bell. Clay was helped to his stool, eyes glazed. In all probability, he would have recovered in the regular 60-second rest period – his powers of recuperation were phenomenal- but trainer Angelo Dundee wanted to make certain. He noticed a rip in one of Clay's gloves, from which poked a small tuft of padding. Dundee, by his own admission, opened it up even more. The rules of boxing are strict: gloves must be in good condition. It took almost an extra minute for the replacement glove to be found and put on.

Clay, head clear, began round five with a

lightning barrage of jabs. He reopened a cut over Cooper's left eye, which got wider and wider, and soon blood was everywhere, the smell of it carried across the auditorium on the damp night air. The wild crowd began begging the referee to end the fight. By now Cooper could hardly see. The actress Elizabeth Taylor screamed 'Stop it! Stop it!' from her ringside seat. Clay threw in two more jabs, Cooper's head jarring under their impact. Referee Tommy Little stepped in and stopped the match. Cooper, nearly blinded by blood, did not argue. Clay's prediction had come true. When his gloves came off he held up one hand to the booing crowd, showing the 'five' he had forecast.

Among those in the stadium watching Clay was Jack Nilon, manager of Sonny Liston, the world heavyweight champion. Afterwards

Nilon went along to Clay's dressing room with a message from Liston: 'He says to please drink your orange juice and your milk shakes. Stay well and healthy. You talked yourself into a world title fight.'

THE CHAMPION

Few thought Clay had a prayer against Liston. Clay was too young, too immature. More to the point, Liston was too good, too strong. His fists were a fearsome 15 inches in circumference, the biggest of any champion. It had taken him a mere 2 minutes 6 seconds to defeat Floyd Patterson in 1962 for the title. Charles 'Sonny' Liston, the ex-stick-up artist who had learned to box in the penitentiary, was a monster. His big jabs would shut 'The Mouth' for good.

There was, though, one person who thought Clay would beat Liston: Cassius Marcellus Clay Jr himself. He endlessly taunted Liston, driving a bus around America across the top of which had been painted (by his father, of course): 'CASSIUS CLAY – WORLD'S MOST COLORFUL FIGHTER'. Under that was: 'LISTON MUST GO IN 8'. Clay's jibes got to the 'Big Ugly Bear'. When the two men accidentally met in a casino, Liston slapped Clay across the face for 'being too damn fresh'.

The fight was set for 25 February 1964 in Miami. Clay turned up for the morning weigh-in wearing a blue denim jacket with 'Bear Hunting' written across the back. He was flanked by the revered black middleweight Sugar Ray Robinson and his own aide Drew 'Bundini' Brown. The assembled press thought Clay had gone crazy with pre-fight tension. Sighting Liston he screamed, 'You are too ugly. You are a bear. I'm going to whup you so bad. You're a chump.' Clay then began chanting a couplet composed by Bundini, 'Float like a butterfly, sting like a bee'. Local officials fined him for misconduct. A doctor took his pulse and found it had gone up from its normal 54 beats a minute to 120. The physician announced gravely that Clay was 'scared to death'. The odds makers had Liston as 7–1 favourite.

Clay's histrionic act – for an act is what it was – had the desired effect on Liston. The champion was prepared for no more than a three-round contest when he entered the ring against 'the faggot' at Miami Beach Auditorium that evening.

At nine p.m., the bell sounded for round one. And Clay commenced to dance – like a butterfly. Every time Liston threw a punch, Clay floated away. The champion started to get angry, and something like murder settled on his face. By midway through round three Liston was breathing hard, and Clay had started to jab, hesitantly at first, then harder and faster. Just before the bell, with Liston against the ropes, Clay put in a flurry of punches, one of which tore a big gash under the champion's left eye.

Liston's performance continued to deteriorate during round four. And then, suddenly, Clay was having trouble with his own eyes, blinking, pawing at them with his gloves. At the end of the fourth he stumbled to his corner and said to Angelo Dundee: 'There's something in my eyes. I can't see properly. I want to quit.'

Clay's parents at the World Heavyweight Championship, 1964

'No way', Dundee snapped. 'Get in there and fight,' and he literally shoved the protesting Clay out for the fifth round.

The 'something' blinding Clay is usually thought to have been liniment used on Liston's shoulder finding its way into the contender's eyes. According to some sources the truth is more repulsive. Liston made a deliberate attempt to blind Clay, smearing a 'special potion' on his gloves from a tube carried by his cutman,. But though Clay was virtually sightless in round five, Liston was still unable to dispose of him.

When Clay came out for round six, his eyes had cleared and victory was in sight. He dazzled Liston with pinpoint punches. The bigger man's legs and arms seemed to seize up. At the bell for the close of the round,

Liston stumbled over to his corner and flopped on to his stool.

And then, when the bell sounded for round seven, Liston simply stayed where he was. 'That's it,' he growled. For a second there was confusion. Clay was the first to realize what was happening, and jumped up and down. Liston was a beaten man.

Officials poured into the ring. Clay fought his way through them, climbed like a squirrel on to the red velvet ropes and held his still-gloved hand aloft before the rows of seats occupied by the press. 'Eat your words,' he howled. 'Eat your words.'

Cassius Marcellus Clay Jr was champion of the world.

Allegedly, Liston capitulated because of bursitis in his shoulder. There was no such injury. He feared being totally humiliated. It was better to surrender hurt.

As the new champion, Clay was ready to make a momentous annoucement to America. The very day after his triumph he admitted that he was a member of the Black Muslims, the most militant of the civil rights movements then at work in the United States.

BLACK POWER

The conversion of Cassius Clay to Islam and Black Power was no gimmick, but a sincere spiritual and political progression. It had started in 1960 in his home town of Louisville. Despite being Olympic champion he had been refused service in a restaurant because he was black. In disgust, he had thrown his gold medal into the Ohio River. Not long afterwards, he had met the Nation of Islam, headed by the prophet the Honourable Elijah Muhammad, and saw in them the liberation of black people from slavery and subjugation. Clay had been personally admitted to the movement by the Nation of Islam's most famous minister, the charismatic Malcolm X. To mark his conversion, the boxer rid himself of his 'slave name', changing it to 'Cassius X', the X standing for the unknown family name of his African ancestors. Four weeks after winning the world title he changed his name again, this time to Muhammad Ali.

The reaction was swift, and predictable. Many whites – even many blacks – thought the Nation of Islam a dangerous, white-hating sect. More hostility was to come. America was already embroiled in the Vietnam War, its youth subject to the draft. In March 1964 Ali was given a deferment by the Draft Board, after he failed the Armed Forces

Qualifying Test. There was uproar. A racist 'Draft That Nigger Clay' campaign was started up by a Georgia lawyer, and the Louisville Draft Board was bombarded by over 1000 petitions and missives demanding that 'Clay' be called up. A typical one read: 'How much has Clay paid you to keep him out of the Army? You had better resign before some soldier takes a shot at you. You are nothing but a yellow-belly Negro lover . . .' In time the Louisville Board would reclassify Ali as fit for service – beginning the chain of events which would see him stripped of his title – but before then there was still some boxing to be done.

The contract for the Liston–Clay bout had a return clause, which was set for November 1964 in Boston. Fan wisdom was that Ali had won the title by a fluke, and a rematch would be the end of the Black Muslim loudmouth. To make sure it was so, Liston – never a natural for gym work – immediately threw himself in to training. Visitors to his camp said he was fitter and meaner than ever.

Ali, meanwhile, on the 14 August 1964 married Sonji Roi, a beautiful half-black woman, in Gary, Indiana. Together they toured Africa, where Ali shook the hands of a number of heads of state.

The world title holder returned weighing 245 pounds, his heaviest to date, the physical embodiment of a heavyweight champion. He radiated confidence.

And then, just three days before the Liston fight, disaster struck. Sparring with Jimmy

Ellis (later to become world heavyweight champ himself), Ali took a heavy low blow and suffered a double hernia. He was rushed to hospital and the Liston bout was postponed.

More problems followed. Because of Ali's conversion to the Muslim faith and his draft deferment, venue's all over America refused to host the rescheduled match. Finally, an offer came in from the small, drab, unknown town of Lewiston, Maine. The promoters grabbed it.

At 10.30 p.m. on the evening of 25 May 1965, Sonny Liston and Muhammad Ali stood eyeball to eyeball in the high school ice hockey rink in Lewiston. Two minutes later it was all over, and Ali walked the ring with his arms held high in triumph.

What exactly happened in those 120 seconds is still controversial. Moments into the opening round, Liston flopped to the canvas after taking what has become known as Ali's 'phantom punch'. The referee, Jersey Joe Walcott, failed to pick up the timekeeper's count and permitted the fight to continue, despite the fact that well over 10 seconds had elapsed before Liston regained his feet. Eventually alerted to his error by Nat Fleischer of *Ring Magazine*, Walcott stopped the fight. Fans began shouting 'Fix! Fix!'

Most people were convinced that Liston had thrown the fight. There even grew up a rumour that he had been visited beforehand by a couple of Black Muslims who promised him a bullet if he won.

In fact, as an examination of the film of the

fight shows, Ali caught Liston on the jaw with a perfect punch. It was so fast that Liston never saw it coming and was therefore mentally unprepared for the shock of its impact.

The victory certified Ali's greatness. But there was no shortage of contenders who wanted the crown off his head, some of them for other than pugilistic reasons. Two-time world heavyweight champion Floyd Patterson published a letter in newspapers criticizing Ali and the Black Muslims. 'I am willing to fight', Patterson said, 'just so I can bring the championship back to America.' The sentiment was well received by white Americans, and Patterson became the first black 'White Hope' in boxing.

The hope did not last long. Patterson – who

had been twice KO'd by Liston – went into the ring against Ali on 22 November 1965 in Las Vegas. Ali danced and held his hands down, inviting Patterson to hit him. Patterson could not. After twelve rounds, the referee ended the humiliation. Ali was still The Champ.

Three months after the Patterson fight Ali, relaxing on his Miami lawn, was informed by a reporter that the pass–percentile mark for the armed forces test had been dropped to 15, and that Ali had been reclassified 1-A – fit for service. Asked for his reaction, Ali replied, 'I ain't got no quarrels with them Vietcongs.' Within hours the headline across America was that Ali was a 'TOOL OF HANOI'.

All major cities in the US banned Ali from fighting within their limits. Even hick towns.

Ali fights Floyd Patterson, November 1965

Ali had no choice but to go abroad to fight. After demolishing George Chuvalo in Canada at the end of March 1966, he went to London, and in May defeated the easy-bleeding Henry Cooper again, plus the luckless Brian London in August. In Germany, also in August, the southpaw Karl Mildenberger was retired in round twelve. Ali had beaten the best that Europe could offer. There was nowhere left to go but back to the USA in the hope that some venue would open its doors.

One did. On the evening of 16 November 1966 Ali stepped into the ring at the Houston Astrodome. His opponent was Cleveland Williams, a big powerful boxer who had once given Liston a tough fight. That night, Ali was magical. In the first round, the challenger was unable to land a single punch on the

Training to fight Brian London, 1966

dancing champion. In round two, Ali mesmerized with his feet – the famous 'Ali Shuffle' – then flattened Williams with a left hook. A series of rapid-fire left and right jabs put Williams down on the canvas in round three. Those who said Ali couldn't punch winced in embarrassment.

After Williams, the next contender to try his chances was the giant Ernie Terrell, who had infuriated Ali by persistently calling him 'Clay'. 'What's my name?', Ali muttered, throughout the fight (again in the Houston Astrodome, on 16 February 1967), 'tell me, what's my name?' Terrell, bloodied and battered, learned it the hard way. Ali's fights were no longer straightforward ring rumbles. Every time he went into the ring he had the pride of his race and his beliefs to defend. Winning was more important than ever. A

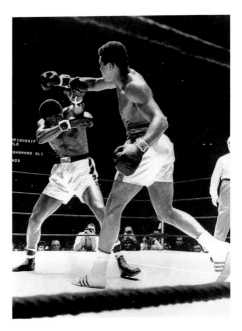

Ali and Terrell, 1967

cause lay on his shoulders. Ali could have disposed of Terrell as early as round eight. He prolonged the fight for the full fifteen rounds, still shouting at Terrell, 'What's my name?'

Just over six weeks later, on 22 March, Ali again defended his title against a top contender. (It could never be said that Ali ducked the tough opponents.) This was the 34-year-old Zora Folley, a veteran of many contests. Against Ali, however, his surname proved apt. From the outset of the fight at Madison Square Garden he was outclassed by Ali's speed of hand and foot. The merciful end came in round six with a crunching blow to the jaw.

Muhammad Ali was the undisputed King of the Ring.

Only three weeks later, however, the King lost his crown. Not to a boxer, but to a far tougher opponent. The US Establishment.

EXILE

The morning of 28 April 1967. At the
Induction Center on San Jacinto Street,
Houston, a voice calls out: 'Cassius Clay –
Army.'

Ali does not take the necessary step forward.
He refuses to join the armed forces. He cites
his religion as the reason (the Nation of Islam
is pacifist).

The reaction was immediate. The World

Boxing Association stripped him of his title.

Soon afterwards he was brought before the courts, sentenced to five years in jail and fined $100,000. He was freed pending an appeal, but prevented from practising his profession. To ensure that he did not box abroad, the US Government took his passport.

Soon Ali, who had earned millions in the ring, was in serious financial trouble. One major expense was legal fees, another was alimony: he and Sonji had divorced just ten months after their wedding, when she found that she was unable to accept the Muslim code which banned women from smoking and wearing cosmetics. Since then Ali had married again, this time to Belinda Boyd, a Black Muslim from Chicago.

As a means of making money, Ali began speaking at colleges – he was the third most sought-after speaker in the US, after Senators Edmund Muskie and Edward Kennedy – and even took to the stage as a Broadway actor in the play, *Buck White*. Another venture was the 'Champburger' chain of fast food restaurants. It collapsed.

He regretted nothing. Throughout his long exile, he remained sure he had made the correct decision that day at the Draft Board in Houston. Asked if he missed boxing, he replied, 'No. Boxing misses me.'

Ali was right. The boxing authorities found new heavyweight champions in Jimmy Ellis and Joe Frazier, but the fight game had lost its main attraction.

For three years the only bout Ali fought was in a computer program. In 1969 a US company fed all available statistics on Ali and Rocky Marciano into a computer to find the all time greatest. The computer chose Marciano by a KO in round thirteen. As Ali humorously pointed out, 'The computer was made in Alabama'; it was unlikely, therefore, to give a black boy a break.

By this time much of America had become uneasy about the war in Vietnam. Perceptions had shifted – in Ali's direction. Young Americans burnt their draft cards and chanted 'Hell, no, we won't go.' Older Americans were coming around to the same viewpoint. Suddenly, Ali's stance seemed less controversial. There was guilt too, for the way he had been punished for his religious beliefs in a supposedly democratic country.

And there was respect. Ali had put his money where his mouth was. He had walked out on millions of dollars because of what he believed in. As opinion softened, so there came the first glimmerings of a willingness to let him box again.

Atlanta, Georgia, a city where blacks had political clout, was the first to relent. On 16 October 1970 Ali fought the white boxer Jerry Quarry in a dilapidated Atlanta stadium full of adulatory black 'beautiful people'. Quarry was disposed of in round three with eye damage.

Ali, 'The People's Champion', as he termed himself, was back.

But another champion had arisen during his exile from the ring, the former slaughterhouse worker Joe Frazier, now the World Boxing Association heavyweight title-holder. With Ali relicensed, it was inevitable that he and Frazier should be matched.

And so it happened, the most widely discussed and awaited fight of all time, scheduled for 8 March 1971. For participating in what simply became known as 'The Fight', Ali and Frazier were guaranteed 2.5 million dollars each, the richest purse in boxing history.

THE FIGHT

In the build-up to The Fight, Ali used his old psyching trick of writing off Frazier before the event. Asked what chance Frazier had, Ali replied: 'Slim and none.' The experts, though, gave Frazier their support. He was younger, and Ali had been laid off for some of his best years. Since his bout against Quarry Ali had only fought once, against the Argentinian champion Oscar Bonavena in New York on 7 December 1970. Ali had won, but he had looked ominously slow in the leg.

The Fight was held at Madison Square Garden on 8 March 1971, before a celebrity-studded audience which included Frank Sinatra and astronaut Alan Shepard, the first American in space. As expected Ali came out fast, skipping around the ring in his German-made shuffle shoes. He jabbed at the lumbering Frazier, but was unable to do him damage, despite a longer reach. Frazier, machine-like, unstoppable, simply kept marching forwards. Once Ali's speed went, in round four, he was in trouble. Frazier caught him against the ropes and threw a series of vicious punches. Ali fell back on psychology. He smiled at the crowd, as if to say 'This is not hurting me. Is this the best Frazier can do?' As the fight progressed, Ali took longer and longer rests against the ropes, absorbing Frazier's murderous punches. By the tenth, Ali had done his best work and Frazier, his face raised in thick welts and bruises, had forced himself ahead on points. Reaching deep down into the well, Ali staged a good fourteenth. But the last round brought the bitter, irrevocable moment of defeat. A left hook from Frazier sprawled Ali flat. He got up – no one could say he lacked courage – and finished The Fight on his feet, but his right cheek bulged damagingly. All three officials scored Frazier the winner.

Suddenly, 'The Greatest' looked like a has-been. He fought some more fights after Frazier but failed to impress. In 1972 Ali's pugilistic use-by-date seemed confirmed absolutely when, on 31 March, in San Diego, the comparatively unknown Ken Norton broke his jaw. The only good news to go Ali's way in over two years was when, on 29 June 1971, the Supreme Court had quashed his conviction for draft dodging.

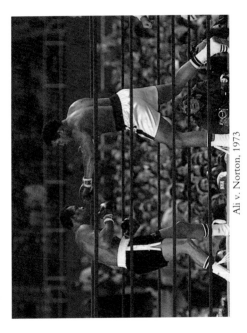

Ali v. Norton, 1973

And then Ali began to achieve things in the ring which were more than amazing, they were unbelievable.

On 28 January 1974 Ali again met Frazier at Madison Square Garden. Frazier had recently lost his title to the giant George Foreman and needed to prove that he was still a contender. Ali needed to prove that he was still a credible fighting force. To the astonishment of the fight pundits and fans, Ali turned in a scintillating performance, with all the speed and skill of old. In the second round, Ali hit Frazier with a perfect straight right. Frazier wobbled, but was saved by the bell. In the seventh, Frazier hit Ali so hard he dazed him, and Ali had to box hard to survive the round. After that, Ali piled on the points and won a deserved decision. The memory slate of his earlier defeat by Joe Frazier was wiped clean.

The win qualified Ali for the dubious distinction of being the next challenger to George Foreman, the seemingly invincible world heavyweight champion, arguably the most ferocious puncher of all time.

Ali meets Frazier again, 1974

THE RUMBLE IN THE JUNGLE

Shortly before dawn on Wednesday, 30 October 1974, some 70,000 Africans and a worldwide selection of pressmen gathered in the soccer stadium at Kinshasa in the African state of Zaire. The strange hour for the Foreman–Ali fight was dictated by the TV needs of the US companies underwriting the fight (New York is six hours behind), a present to the people of Zaire – formerly the Republic of the Congo – on the occasion of their independence. The purse was a mammoth 10 million dollars.

Even Ali's keenest supporters did not think he could win. After all, Foreman had pulverized Frazier and Norton, and Ali had worked hard against both. Archie Moore, Ali's one-time trainer, by then the manager of Foreman, wrote Ali a letter expressing his belief that Foreman might actually kill him, adding an Ali-type rhyme as a postscript: 'You've gotten too old/To win the Big Gold.'

But Ali radiated confidence. Warming up as the fight was about to begin, he shouted down from the ring to one commentator. 'Think this old nigger has got any chance of beating me?' and waved his white-bandaged hands in mock fear.

The fight against Foreman, Kinshasa, 1974

The fight was unforgettable. It seemed that Ali's one slim chance was to stay away from Foreman's punches and dance, dance, dance. He did the opposite. Ali began the first round by going straight at a perplexed Foreman and throwing a series of right punches. He then retired to the ropes and actually invited Foreman to hit him. Foreman obliged. 'You punch like a sissy,' Ali retorted.

The pattern did not alter through rounds two and three. Foreman punching, Ali lying on the ropes (what he called 'rope-a-dope') commentating on the poorness of Foreman's punching and taunting him: 'You got twelve more rounds of this sucker.'

In the fifth Foreman made a gigantic effort, unleashing two left hooks which pounded Ali's head. The challenger stayed on his feet.

Then he came off the ropes to thunder Foreman's head apart. Foreman, at the close of the round, staggered to his stool and slumped. Meanwhile, Ali declined his stool and waved on the crowd with a chant in the local dialect, 'Ali – boom-aye-yay!' ('Ali – knock him down and kill him!').

For two more rounds, Ali let Foreman wear himself out in the oppressive heat of the African night. Ali had saved up a final impertinence. He lay on the ropes in round eight, then pushed Foreman out to where he could hit him with a perfect combination, finishing with a long, looping right to his opponent's jaw. Foreman crashed like an axed tree and failed to beat the count.

At thirty-two Ali was champion again. He had equalled Floyd Patterson's record of

Ali and Bugner, Kuala Lumpur, 1974

winning the heavyweight title twice. As he left the ring, he shouted at Foreman's manager Archie Moore, 'Too old am I, Archie?'

The next morning Ali, almost unmarked by the fight, took a walk. He was accosted by a wide-eyed group of playing boys who wanted to box with him. He sparred gently and when one tiny boy planted his fist in Ali's stomach, the champion grunted and fell to the floor. For the only time in his life, the count of ten was tolled over Muhammad Ali – by laughing children. Ali rose and shook hands with his opponent and said, 'You can tell everybody you just whupped the greatest heavyweight champion of all time.' Ali's greatness did not just extend to his prowess in the ring, but went far beyond it.

In the nine months after Zaire, Ali knocked off Chuck Wepner and Ron Lyle inside the distance and then, in July 1975, laboured to win a dull, well-paid encounter with Joe Bugner in Malaysia. There was more to come, however – another superb fight with Joe Frazier. A deep personal feud had grown up between the two men. This time they would settle it, once and for all – who *was* The Greatest?

Ali with Veronica and baby Hana, 1977

THE THRILLA IN MANILA

The third Ali–Frazier super-fight was staged in the Filipino capital, Manila, in the autumn of 1975. Ali brought his entire entourage of fifty people with him. Some were undoubted parasites, but many were sincere friends and helpers. These included Herbert Muhammad, the son of the Nation of Islam's leader and Ali's manager since the expiry of his contract with the Louisville group of businessmen, trainer Angelo Dundee, cornerman Drew 'Bundini' Brown, Ali's doctor Ferdie

Ali fights Spinks, 1978

Pacheco, the physical conditioner Luis Sarria, and Ali's great friend, the photographer Howard Bingham.

Also in the entourage was Veronica Porche, soon to become his third wife.

On the night of 30 September 1975, in Quezon City, on the outskirts of Manila, Ali and Frazier fought the hardest fight ever seen in the professional ring. In the first five rounds Ali pounded Frazier. In the succeeding rounds, Frazier beat Ali's guard to shell his ribs and head. 'I felt close to death,' Ali said later, 'and wanted to quit in the tenth.' Bundini yelled at Ali: 'Force yourself, champ! Go down into the well once more!' Ali did, and gave Frazier an awesome pounding. At the end of the fourteenth Frazier's trainer, Eddie Futch, refused to let his fighter go on.

Muhammad Ali

Ali had won. Afterwards, *Ring* magazine ran a petition declaring that these two magnificent pugilists should never fight each other again.

It would have been wise for Ali to have retired at this point. He had done it all and more. But he carried on, although the road could only lead over the hill. After a round of defences against mediocre challengers, he lost his crown to a young novice, Leon Spinks, who had fought only seven professional bouts. Ali conceded his loss with gentlemanly grace. But on 15 September 1978, he took back the title with a masterful display of boxing, clearly out-pointing Spinks. This made Ali the first man to win boxing's greatest prize three times.

Yet Ali's skills were clearly eroded by age, while his stomach flabbed over his trunks. His

With patients at a children's hospital

hands were so damaged that he could not fight without shots of novocaine in them. On 2 October 1980, in Las Vegas, Larry Holmes gave Ali a bad beating. After ten rounds Angelo Dundee called a halt. 'That's all,' said Dundee. 'The ballgame's over.'

It wasn't quite. Ali fought one more bout, a shambling affair against Trevor Berbick on 11 December 1981 in Nassau. Berbick won.

And then Ali did what his friends and fans wanted him to do. He finally hung up his gloves.

Retirement has been good for Muhammad Ali, despite his much publicized Parkinson's disease, which has at times badly affected his speech and muscular co-ordination. He is

Ali and his son Asad

happily married to his fourth wife, Lonnie, who handles his business affairs. Ali delights in the company of his eight children from his marriages, and his one adopted child. He amuses himself – and his family and friends – in his spare time by performing conjuring tricks.

Religion remains a great influence in his life, and he is still a great fighter for social and racial justice. He travels the globe as an ambassador for these causes, and everywhere attracts huge audiences. He is probably the most famous face in the world. (And, he would no doubt say, 'the prettiest'.)

Muhammad Ali. He made black people proud to be black and gave them the courage to be the equal of whites. Nelson Mandela has written of the inspiration he found in the person of Ali.

And as a boxer, as an exponent of the 'sweet science', Ali was truly what he always said he was.

The Greatest.

FURTHER MINI SERIES
INCLUDE

THEY DIED TOO YOUNG

Elvis
James Dean
Buddy Holly
Jimi Hendrix
Sid Vicious
Marc Bolan
Ayrton Senna
Marilyn Monroe
Jim Morrison

THEY DIED TOO YOUNG

Malcolm X
Kurt Cobain
River Phoenix
John Lennon
Glenn Miller
Isadora Duncan
Rudolph Valentino
Freddie Mercury
Bob Marley

FURTHER MINI SERIES
INCLUDE

HEROES OF THE WILD WEST

General Custer
Butch Cassidy and the Sundance Kid
Billy the Kid
Annie Oakley
Buffalo Bill
Geronimo
Wyatt Earp
Doc Holliday
Sitting Bull
Jesse James